STEVE HAUER

ONE INCH BETWEEN
LIFE AND DEATH

UPDATED AND REVISED SECOND EDITION

For permission requests or inquiries, please contact:

Steven A. Hauer

oneinchstory.com

Contents

Dedication

To my children Jacob Hauer, Claire Hauer, and Nicholaus Bornstein, the greatest blessings God has ever given me. May you walk in faith, dream, and always listen to the quiet voice within. You are my purpose, my light, and my legacy. Thank you for buying *One Inch Between Life and Death Updated and Revised Second Edition*. If you enjoyed the story, please leave a review. It helps others discover the book.

Steven A. Hauer

How It All Began

Before *One Inch Between Life and Death Updated and Revised Second Edition* ever became a book, it was a short story I wrote in high school. I was not trying to become a writer or to make sense of my near-death experience. I was just trying to pass English. It was the end of my junior year, and I was in danger of failing. My English teacher, Mr. Jackson, offered me a chance to earn extra credit by writing a story.

With the help of my special education teacher, Ms. Foote, I wrote about the one thing that had changed my life forever, the accident. Ms. Foote worked with me, helping me make sure every sentence was clear and every "i" and "t" was crossed.

I can still remember sitting in front of one of the very first Apple computers, typing out each word. Recalling the specific model eludes me; however, it was fresh, rendering computer-assisted composition seem like something from the future. When I turned it in, Mr. Jackson smiled and told me how proud he was. He said he had found only one minor error. I had forgotten to end one sentence with a period and quotation mark. That single missing dot became a lasting reminder that even when you aim for perfection, it is the effort that matters most.

After reading my essay, Mr. Jackson encouraged me to enter it into The High School Writer of Minnesota, which was holding a statewide writing contest. The winning entry would receive a ten-thousand-dollar scholarship to a college in North Dakota, which I believe was Jamestown College. I entered the contest, not thinking much of it. Writing was never something I planned to do with my life. At the beginning of my senior year, I was called down to the principal's office. I walked in nervously, unsure of what to expect, and there stood Principal McDermott with a big smile on his face. He congratulated me on winning the scholarship. I was shocked. Writing held no genuine interest during that period.

My plan was to attend trade school, not college. Still, I was grateful and honored, even if I did not fully understand the significance then. Years went by, and I would occasionally share my story with friends or people I met along the way. Almost everyone who heard it told me the same thing, that I should write a book. I always laughed it off and said I was not interested. Writing still did not feel like my path.

That changed approximately ten years ago. While I was in therapy, my therapist suggested that I start writing my story down. Initially, I intended it to help me process everything that had happened. But as I wrote, something deeper took shape. The more I wrote, the more I realized my story was not just about survival. It was about purpose. Sharing my experience touched others in ways I had not expected. People told me my words helped them face their own struggles, gave them hope, or reminded them to hold on to faith when life felt unbearable. That was when I finally understood.

God had given me this story for a reason. I was spared for a purpose. I was not just fortunate to be alive. Furthermore, I am a walking miracle with a story to share. And that story Became One Inch Between Life and Death., Steven A. Hauer (Newspaper clipping reprinted with permission. Some identifying details have been redacted for privacy.)

Introduction

Life can change in an instant. Sometimes, it is a single moment, a single decision, or a single inch that separates life from death. For me, that moment came when I least expected it, during what was supposed to be an ordinary day spent with friends. I never imagined that day would become the turning point of my life. When I began writing this book, I did not create a story for sympathy or attention. I wrote it because my experience was real, and

I felt called to share it. I hope readers find strength, faith, and gratitude in these pages. No matter the trials, perceive that the gloomiest periods offer light, and that divine favor is near. This is not just my story. It is a reminder that each of us walks a path filled with both trials and blessings. It is a story about second chances, about the thin line that separates fear from faith, and about learning to see purpose where there once was pain.

Steven A. Hauer

Sunday Just Hanging Out With Friends

Boys spending a Sunday afternoon together.

The afternoon had started light and carefree, just three boys passing time outdoors. But something shifted as the sun dipped lower, stretching long shadows across the trees. The birds, once playful, now seemed cautious. Their cheerful chirping turned into uneasy calls. The excitement of the day faded, leaving a strange weight in my chest. Just then, my brother-in-law Joe appeared at the back door of the house.

"Boys, come in for lunch," he called. His tone was serious, and we exchanged curious glances before heading inside. Kurt sighed, tired of sharing his dad's rifle. "Hey, don't your brothers have a 22 rifle you could borrow?" he asked. I shook my head. "No, they don't enjoy lending them out." Kurt leaned forward, eyes lighting up with a new idea. "Then let's go for squirrels instead. Do you know any good spots?" I thought for a moment. "The Winters Woods has some, but it's hit or miss. Larson's Woods would be better if we don't get caught." Chris frowned. "Winter's is too thick with brush. You can't find anything in there." "Yeah," I admitted, "but there's always Larson's Woods. Plenty of squirrels there." Then, an idea came to me. "Wait, Joe's dad might have a 22 rifle we can borrow. Maybe he'll ask if we can help him out for a bit." Kurt's grin widened. "Now you're talking." Excited, I went to find Joe, who was washing dishes at the sink.

A Boy aiming a firearm in the woods

"Hey, do you think we could borrow a 22 rifle to do some hunting?" Joe shook his head. "No, Steve, I don't."

Disappointment set in, but before I could leave, he added, "Tell you what, if you help me move some pigs at my dad's place, I'll ask him." I did not want to do it, but the trade seemed fair.

"How long will it take?" "Fifteen, maybe thirty minutes. Then we'll see about the rifles." That was good enough for me. I returned to tell the guys.

"We can get the rifles, but we've got to help move some pigs first." Kurt was in right away. Chris groaned. "Every time we go over there, we end up doing chores." "I get it," I said, "but Joe swore it'd be quick. And then we get to shoot with a real 22 rifle. Worth it, right?" Chris hesitated, then nodded. As we walked toward Joe's car, the air felt heavier somehow. Perhaps the clouds, which thickened in the distance, or something deeper evaded explanation. We were just kids seeking adventure, but somewhere deep inside, I felt that by the time the sun set, this day would be one I would never forget.

Moving The Pigs

The 1983 Pontiac Le Mans was the car we drove.

The midday sun beat down on us as we stood in the dusty pen, staring at the stubborn sow. She was not going anywhere. She planted her hooves in the dirt, and her body stiffened with defiance. "Come on, girl," Joe muttered, wiping sweat from his forehead. We pushed, pulled, and coaxed, but the pig refused to move. She was big, strong, and uninterested in our plans. Frustration built with every passing minute. The harder we tried, the more determined she became. Just when it seemed like we had her under control, she bolted, darting off in the wrong direction. "Block her!" Joe shouted. Kurt and Chris scrambled to cut her off while I grabbed a large sheet of plywood, holding it in front of me like a shield. With a few sharp turns, firm nudges, and a lot of shouting, we steered her back toward the pen. She grunted in protest but gave in, trotting into her enclosure at last. We stood there catching our breath, sweat dripping down our backs. Kurt panted, "That was ridiculous."

Chris laughed, shaking his head. "We'd better get those rifles after this." Joe wiped his hands on his jeans. "Let's find out." He turned to his dad, Lonnie, who had been watching from the shade of the barn.

"The boys want to shoot some blackbirds and check out Johnny Hauer's Woods for squirrels," Joe said. Lonnie raised an eyebrow. "You know it's not squirrel season yet, right? That starts next weekend." "I know," I blurted. "We're just scouting spots. That way I won't get skunked on opening day." Lonnie studied us for a long moment before nodding.

"Alright. But don't shoot any squirrels. You'd get a big fine, and they'd take your hunting privileges away." "We won't!" the three of us said in unison. Satisfied, Lonnie disappeared into the house. A few minutes later, he returned carrying two 22 rifles. "All I've got are single shots," he said. Chris and I grinned. "That's fine! The prospect of not sharing filled us with delight. I turned to Joe. "Could we borrow your car?" I said. "I thought you were hunting in Johnny Hauer's Woods?" "We are," I said, "but we want to enter from the north side. It's too far to walk. I figured we could drive up Johnny Hauer's field driveway." Joe hesitated, then sighed. "Alright, but be careful. Don't shoot yourselves or each other.

Remember what you learned in firearm safety training." "We will," we promised. Excitement surged through us as we jumped into Joe's car. We pulled out of Lonnie's farm and drove the short distance to Johnny Hauer's field driveway.

Field dirt road to the woods (fence on the right and plowed dirt field on the left)

As we reached the top of the hill where the woods began, we parked at the edge of the field, grabbed our rifles, and stepped into the trees. The dense underbrush swallowed us. Branches scraped against our arms and faces, and dried leaves crunched beneath our boots. The woods were alive with sound, the rustling of unseen creatures, the distant call of birds, the occasional snap of a twig. We moved, scanning the trees for any signs of movement. "There!" Kurt whispered, pointing. A blackbird sat perched on a low branch, its head tilted as if watching us. Kurt raised his rifle and steadied his breath. A shot rang out, shattering the stillness. The bird shot upward, vanishing into the treetops. "Darn it," Kurt muttered. Before we could react, a blur of motion exploded from the brush. A rabbit, startled by the noise, bolted past us, its white tail flashing as it disappeared into the thicket. Kurt laughed. "Did you see that?" Chris shook his head. "I think you scared it half to death!" We high-fives, the rush of the moment flooding us with adrenaline. Shooting more blackbirds was what we'd been waiting for. With rifles held, we ventured deeper into woods.

The Shot That Changed Everything

Us boys walking through the woods on a quiet Sunday afternoon.

The woods were alive with movement and sound, a quiet symphony only nature knows how to play. The leaves whispered above us, brushing against one another like restless spirits stirred by the wind. Branches swayed and creaked, casting shifting patterns of light and shadow across the woods.

Somewhere ahead, a crow called out, sharp and distant, then vanished into silence again. The three of us moved through the undergrowth, our boots crunching over brittle twigs and damp leaves. Each step felt deliberate, almost sacred, as if the woods demanded we tread with respect. Chris led the way, steady and confident, his eyes scanning the trees. Kurt followed close behind, gripping his rifle a little too, exciting the hunt written all over his face. I brought up the rear, alert and tuned into every sound, the snap of a branch, the flap of wings, the rush of cool air carrying smelling pine and earth. The sun had started its slow descent, pouring golden light between the trunks like liquid fire. The fading daylight imparted unease, though the woods were beautiful, still, and glowing. Kurt froze.

"Over there," he whispered, pointing toward a tangle of branches. I followed his gaze. A blackbird perched low, its head cocked, listening. Chris leaned in.

A squirrel sitting on a branch in the trees.

"Take the shot." Kurt nodded, raised his rifle, and drew a steady breath. We all froze. Then, CRACK! The sharp report of the 22 split the silence wide open. The bird exploded upward, a streak of feathers vanishing into the treetops. "You missed," I said, smirking. Kurt frowned. "No way. That shot was dead on."

Chris shook his head, grinning. "Bird's gone, man. You scared the hell out of it." Kurt sighed and lowered his rifle. "Whatever. Let's keep moving." We pressed deeper into the woods, our laughter fading behind us. The air grew cooler, the light dimmer. Squirrels darted along branches, tails flicking. Every rustle and chirp seemed amplified. Being there offered peace; it was grounding. Out here, it was just us and the world as God made it. As we crossed onto the Larson's' property, the sunlight softened into a warm orange haze. It felt almost like walking through a dream. We spotted squirrels jumping from tree to tree and readied ourselves again. I reminded them to aim high, to keep the bullets buried in the trees and away from the horses grazing below. We weren't reckless, just boys chasing the excitement of the hunt. Gunshots echoed again, scattering the squirrels and sending a thrill down my spine. The woods came alive in motion, wings, branches, heartbeats. It was pure adrenaline, the kind that makes you feel invincible. Then, the first low rumble rolled through the sky. Kurt glanced up. "That thunder?" Another growl answered him, closer this time. I looked west. The sky had turned an eerie gray-green, and the air smelled electric.

"Guys," I said, "we better get going." Chris hesitated. "It's just wind." "No," I said, watching the clouds darken. "We'll get soaked. And we'll have to clean the guns." Lightning flickered on the horizon. The wind picked up, swirling leaves around our legs. By the time we started back through Johnny Hauer's woods, the storm was chasing us. The first bolt cracked through the sky, so bright it burned my vision white. Thunder answered a second later, loud, violent, close. The air roared in our ears. The branches above bent and hissed as if alive. "Come on!" I shouted over the wind. We sprinted to the last segment, sliding through the soggy undergrowth until the vehicle appeared, offering a small refuge from the disorder. We piled inside, breathless and soaked, hearts pounding. Kurt gave a nervous laugh. "That was an adventure."

Chris tried to smile. "Next time, we'll check the weather first." We all chuckled, tension disguised as humor. Outside, the rain came down in sheets. The air smelled of wet dirt and ozone. Kurt said, "Let's just throw the guns in back and wait it out. We don't have to be home until five." Chris and I nodded. We each had single-shot rifles, so we unloaded them and laid them across the back seat. Kurt followed suit, emptying the extra bullets from his pocket. I slid into the driver's seat; Chris sat behind me. Kurt stood outside on the passenger side, fiddling with his gun. "Dang things jammed," he muttered, trying to clear the chamber. He frowned, tugging at it. "Steve, have you got a knife?" I checked my pockets. "No."

"Chris?" He shook his head. "Nothing." The thunder cracked again, deafening this time. Rain splattered against the car roof like pebbles. "Kurt!" I yelled. "Get those bullets out and get in the car!" He nodded, opening the back door across from me. Rain soaked his hair, his shirt clinging to his shoulders. He turned the rifle, chamber half-closed. And then, BANG. The sound was so loud it seemed to split the world in half. For a heartbeat, everything froze. My eyes darted to the dash, expecting a bullet hole. There was none. Then I felt it, the pain. Not just pain, but fire. White-hot, merciless fire ripped through my back and exploded outward. My breath hitched. I tried to speak, but no air came. Every nerve in my body screamed, electricity racing from my toes to my scalp. The world tilted. The car blurred. My hands clawed at the dashboard. I heard voices, distant, panicked, but they sounded like echoes underwater. "Steve!" Chris's voice broke. "Where, where are you hit?" "My…" The word caught in my throat. I forced another breath. "My back." Chris turned, eyes wide with shock. "You shot him! You shot him, Kurt!" Kurt's hands flew to his head. "I didn't, I didn't mean to!" His voice cracked with terror. The tingling spread through me, cold and strange, like my body didn't belong to me anymore. My vision pulsed bright, then dim, then bright again. Somewhere in the chaos, I heard my scream raw, unfiltered, torn from some place deep. Kurt's voice broke through it, frantic, desperate.

"Steve! Steve! Can you hear me?" I turned my head just enough to see his face, pale, trembling, eyes wide as saucers. The look of disbelief and horror on Kurt's face said it all. Then the world faded, the edges of everything softening, like the storm itself was swallowing me whole.

Us boys getting ready to go hunting along the field dirt driveway

Who's Driving

Field driveway with a fence on one side and a plowed road leading down the hill.

Chaos surrounded us. Pain throbbed in my back, my head was spinning, and panic clawed at my thoughts. We needed to get to the hospital fast. Kurt and I argued over who should drive. I insisted I could do it, but Kurt refused. His voice was sharp and desperate.

"I shot you, Steve! You can't drive like this!" I reluctantly gave in. Kurt slid behind the wheel, his hands shaking as he turned the key. The engine sputtered to life, but the rain hammered down, making it nearly impossible to see. Chris, thinking fast, peeled off his sweatshirt. "Steve, lean forward," he said, pressing the fabric against my back. I gritted my teeth, a fresh wave of pain hitting me as he tried to slow the bleeding. In my mind, I could see the quickest way out. Drive forward past the ruts, then back up and make a clean turn toward the road. But Kurt had other plans. Instead of following my directions, he jerked the wheel, trying to turn the car around right where we were. He went into a plowed field, a big mistake. The tires sank deep into the mud, spinning uselessly. The back end entered a dead furrow, resulting in our entrapment. I felt helpless. Frustrated. The pain in my back pulsed with every heartbeat. I couldn't believe it. After everything, we were wasting time sinking into the muddy field. Kurt panicked and shouted, "Chris, get out and push!" "Do not exit the car, Chris," I said. Then I yelled at "Kurt, take your foot off the gas." Kurt followed my command. "Okay, Kurt, straighten out the wheels and punch it." With a loud groan of the engine, the tires finally caught traction. The car lurched forward, fishtailing as Kurt floored it down the driveway.

Too fast. We were barreling down the narrow field path at sixty miles an hour, mud flying from the tires, water streaking across the windshield. The path was nothing more than a rutted strip of dirt cut through an open field, uneven and slick from the rain. My pulse pounded in my ears. I felt everything closing in, pain, fear, and the cold certainty that one wrong move could send us tumbling into the ditch. I squeezed my eyes shut and started whispering the Hail Mary under my breath.

I needed something, anything, to focus on besides the speed

and the shrinking stretch of muddy path ahead. We were flying toward the paved road at the bottom of the hill. But Kurt wasn't slowing down. "Kurt, slow down!" I shouted, my voice raw with panic. He slammed on the brakes.

Too late. The tires skidded. We shot off the field path and across the two lane road, slick with rain and shadowed by the trees overhead. Just then, a car came hurtling down the hill toward us. A fleeting glimpse of metal plus headlights, then, within a blink, finality felt certain. Car Accident Number One. Somehow avoided.

Kurt jerked the wheel hard, and we veered into the ditch. The car dropped with a jarring thud, mud spraying up around us. A jagged tree stump loomed in our path, but Kurt steered hard to the side, narrowly missing it. We tore through the ditch, the tires fighting for traction, bouncing violently over the uneven ground.

House across the road from the field driveway with a tree stump near the ditch.

Somehow miraculously, he guided us up into the neighbor's driveway. I didn't know how we were still upright. I didn't know how we were still alive. But we weren't safe yet. Kurt threw the car into reverse, trying to rush me to the hospital.

That was when car accident number two nearly happened. Another vehicle was coming from the opposite direction, its bumper already crossing the yellow line, headed straight for us. For a breathless second, all I could see was that car, the rain slicked road, and the dizzying space between us and a head on collision. The same hill. The same blind hill.

Seconds, maybe inches, between survival and something far worse. Silence. I sat there, chest heaving, trying to catch my breath. The body held pain, while my mind grappled with recent events. We had come within inches of dying. Kurt, still gripping the wheel, looked shaken. His face was pale, his breaths unsteady. However, we weren't safe yet.

"Kurt, look both ways before backing out," I warned as he threw the car into reverse. He didn't. "Kurt, stop!" I screamed. A blur of motion. A car whizzed past, our bumper barely over the yellow line, missing the vehicle.

My stomach dropped. Second car accident missed We almost got hit. Again. Kurt sat frozen, realization finally sinking in. His fingers clenched the wheel, his eyes locked on the road. I exhaled slowly, trying to steady my nerves. "Kurt, you have to be more careful," I said, my voice tight with anger and fear. "You could have gotten us all killed." He nodded, swallowing hard. He knew. It woke both of us in that instance. It reminded us of the dangers of driving and the importance of staying alert and focused on the road. We will never forget this lesson. It will remain with us every time we get behind the wheel. As we drove off, I couldn't help but feel grateful that we had narrowly escaped disaster, and hopeful that Kurt and I would never make that same mistake again.

Turning to Kurt, I demanded an explanation for his reckless driving. He muttered to me he was trying to get me to the hospital, his gaze conveying desperation. The gravity of the situation hit me like a ton of bricks. Time pressed upon us, and my existence was at risk.

First near miss on the road, moments before we shot across the road and into the ditch.

Car backing out onto the road as another vehicle comes down the hill. Another accident voided.

The Drive To The Hospital

The house I grew up in.

As Kurt accidentally veered toward my parents' house, the chaos and tension of the moment gave way to disbelief at our narrow escapes from disaster. My heart raced with mixed emotions. Part of me was relieved that this wrong turn might bring help faster, but another part of me worried about what would happen next. Kurt's face changed as realization struck. He slowed down, clearly intending to turn around, but something in me urged him to keep driving toward my parents' house.

That instant brought a strange calm, almost like a God presence watched me. When we finally pulled into my parents' driveway, the tension in the air was thick. Kurt and Chris jumped out of the car, grabbed their guns, and ran into the house shouting for help. I sat in the car, pain radiating through my back, waiting for any sign of someone coming. Time seemed to stretch endlessly. Then, through the blur of rain and headlights, I saw movement. My dad, my sister Jane, and my brother-in-law Joe came running outside toward me. The urgency in their movements said everything. Jane quickly took the driver's seat while my dad and Joe climbed into the back, ready to help however they could. The pain in my back was sharp, each breath a reminder of the chaos that had led to this moment. As Jane steered the car through the streets, my mind raced. Fear and pain mixed with a flood of thoughts I couldn't control. I imagined the worst likely scenario: the doctor telling my parents that I smoked. The idea of disappointing them hit me almost as hard as the pain itself. Rain poured harder as we picked up speed. The wipers struggled to keep the windshield clear. Jane switched on the flashers and headlights, doing everything she could to make us visible. We raced down the highway at seventy to eighty miles an hour. The road was wet and slick, the night dark, and the world outside the car seemed to blur together. Other drivers barely noticed. our lights or urgency. No one moved aside. I gripped the seat, praying silently that we would not end up in another accident before reaching the hospital. Fear pressed down on me like the weight of the storm itself. A midst the pain, a midst the chaos, this notion echoed within: Please, God, allow us to arrive there safely.

The Hospital

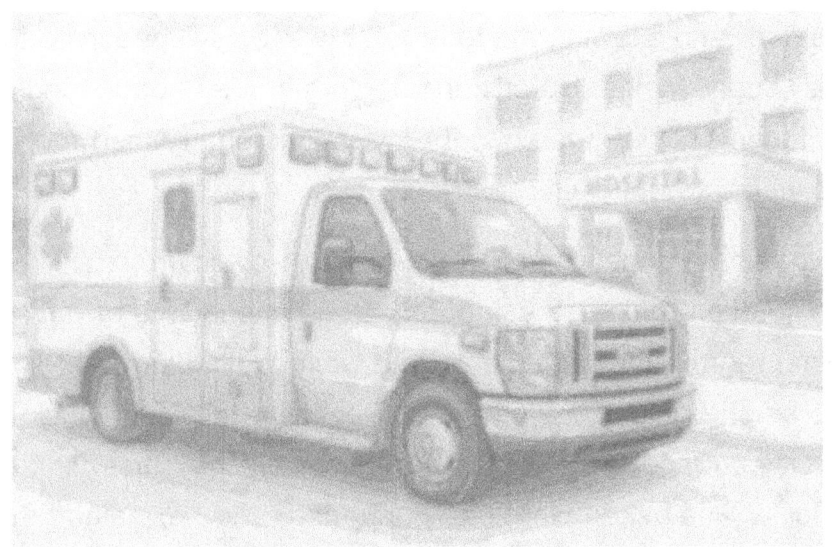

Ambulance near the hospital.

We arrived at Queen of Peace Hospital in New Prague, a small town with a peaceful atmosphere that contrasted with the urgency of our situation. Pulling up to the emergency room entrance, my dad sprang into action. A sense of urgency I had never seen before replaced his calm demeanor. He helped me out of the car as I grimaced in pain, my right side throbbing from the bullet wound. As we approached the emergency room door, a wave of desperation washed over me. I reached out to open the door, only to find it locked.

Panic rose in my chest. I pressed the button for help, and a voice responded, asking how they could help. In that moment of pain and fear, I shouted, "I have been shot!" My words echoed in the empty night. A loud buzzer sounded, unlocking the door and allowing me to enter. My eyes swept across the busy scene inside. Nurses and doctors hurried about, tending to patients. One nurse caught my eye as she rushed toward me with a wheelchair.

With calm urgency, she instructed me to sit down. I sank into the seat, grateful for the support as she pushed me toward an exam room. The bright lights and white walls blurred around me as she guided me onto the examining table. My back hit the icy surface, and I winced at the pain. The nurse worked quickly. She asked what had happened, and I explained that my best friend had accidentally shot me while we were hunting. To my surprise, she conveyed that the hospital lacked personnel to address my situation, and that I'd require transfer to another hospital.

They were preparing for a car accident expected to arrive any minute and couldn't handle both emergencies. She expressed frustration, saying that if we had called ahead, they could have been ready. I felt a mix of confusion and gratitude. I couldn't believe how fast everything had happened. We are going to move to another medical facility. As I lay there waiting, fear took over. My mind jumped to the worst possibilities. Would I need open heart surgery? Would I survive it? Another fear crept in. What if the doctors told my parents I smoked? The thought of their disappointment made my stomach tighten.

A nurse interrupted my thoughts. They needed to take X-rays to determine the severity of my injury and whether surgery was necessary. The news both comforted and terrified me. I silently prayed, calling upon Jesus, the angels, the saints, and all my departed loved ones to help me through this. The nurse told me the images were needed for St. Francis Hospital to understand my condition before the transfer.

As I lay on the cold table, the machine hummed. The clicking echoed through the dimly lit room. I stared at the ceiling, wondering what the images would reveal. Would they show the bullet was close to my heart? Following what appeared to be an eternity, the entrance opened, and the physician entered, his expression serious.

His words hit me hard. "The bullet is dangerously close to your heart, possibly touching it. Survival remains a blessing to you. Two paramedics entered the room with calm efficiency. They transferred me carefully onto the stretcher, reassuring me they would take good care of me.

Adrenaline coursed through my body as they loaded me into the ambulance. They gave me oxygen and pressed gauze against my wound. Hoping to lighten the mood, I asked, "Will you activate the lights and sirens?" I want to get my money's worth." The paramedic sitting beside me laughed. The paramedic inquired, "Are you activating those sirens, flashing those lights?" He continued, "He wants every penny's worth."

When we reached Highway 169, just outside of town, the ambulance suddenly came to a stop. I regarded the paramedic and queried the situation. He described an accident that blocked our route, preventing passage toward the hospital, which existed two blocks distant. I said, "Why don't you take the sidewalk? They perform that way in the movies. We can get there that way."

Both paramedics burst out laughing. The driver called back, "What's so funny?" The paramedic answered, "Steve wants you to drive on the sidewalk like in the movies." The driver laughed again, shaking his head. Finally, we started moving and reached St. Francis Hospital in Shakopee.

As the paramedics rushed me into the emergency room, I noticed the aged walls and worn floors. The room they wheeled me into was massive, filled with bright lights and bustling staff. Six medical workers surrounded me, moving with practiced speed. Two nurses grabbed my arms, trying to start IV lines. I tried to speak through the oxygen mask, but they told me to stay calm.

The nurses exchanged quick glances, struggling to find a vein. Then one of them leaned in and asked quietly, "Do you want to receive your last rites?" The weight of those words hit me like nothing else. Death no longer felt distant. It felt close.

Real. As the nurse prepared to call the priest, I prayed harder than ever before, begging Jesus for mercy.

Moments later, the priest arrived. His gentle voice filled the room with peace as he offered prayers over me. A calm settled over my heart. Just as I began to breathe easier, the doctor entered again. His tone was serious. "Steve, we need to retake the X-rays. The images from Queen of Peace weren't clear. It looks like the bullet may be lodged in your heart." My fear returned instantly, but I replied, "Let's do the X-rays." The nurses helped me to my feet. Every step toward the X-ray room sent waves of pain through my back.

The technician adjusted me into different positions. When she asked me to raise my right arm, I tried but couldn't. A nurse beside me grew impatient and lifted my arm abruptly. Pain shot through my body, and I cried out, "That hurts! Don't ever do that again." The kind technician apologized and guided me back to the exam room. I lay on the cold gurney, staring at the ceiling as the staff disappeared with the images. The silence that followed was heavy and endless. I lay there alone, the weight of everything pressing down on me. I could only pray, hoping I would live to relate this experience.

Surgery or Not

A 22 bullet which is one inch long, one inch away from my heart.

Minutes felt like hours as I lay there, my mind racing with questions about the bullet lodged so close to my heart. The weight of uncertainty pressed down on me harder than the pain itself. What kind of surgery would they need to perform? Would I ever be the same again?

The thought of someone cutting near my heart sent chills down my spine. I could almost feel the invisible line between life and death hovering just above me, daring me to cross it. Every second dragged by, thick with fear. The sterile hum of machines filled the air, a constant reminder that my body had become a battlefield.

I turned to the only source of peace I knew, God. Closing my eyes, I prayed. My voice was silent, but my heart cried out. I pleaded with Jesus Christ to guide the doctors' hands, to give me strength, to let me see my family again. With each whispered prayer, a wave of calm washed over me. The tension in my chest loosened, and I could almost feel His presence wrapping around me like a protective shield.

When I opened my eyes, the fluorescent lights above buzzed, flickering in the corners of the room. The smell of disinfectant hung thick in the air, sharp and sterile. I tried to focus on my breathing, on anything that wasn't fear. The door creaked open, and a tall doctor stepped inside. His expression was serious, but his eyes carried a calm authority. "Steven," he whispered. "How are you feeling?" Before I could answer, he glanced toward my back, inspecting the bandaged wound.

He hesitated, then asked about an earlier incident with one nurse. The memory hit me hard, the nurse asking me to raise my arm too soon, the jolt of pain so intense I'd snapped at her. Shame and frustration mixed in my chest as I explained what had happened. The doctor nodded, his expression softening. "I understand," he said. "Pain can do that to a person." His tone was even, not judging, just human. That small moment of compassion steadied me.

Then he took a breath, preparing to deliver the news I'd been waiting for. "We will not do surgery," he said. For a moment, I thought I'd misheard him. My heart skipped. "What do you mean? Give me the good news then." He folded his arms and explained. "The bullet stopped one inch away from your heart.

Surgery would be more dangerous than leaving it. It's surrounded by tissue now, and removing it could cause more harm than good." I blinked in disbelief. "So, it remains there?"" "For now," he said. "If it ever moves, we'll have to act fast. But it's stable. You're stable." Relief flooded me. I felt lightheaded. I whispered a thank-you to Jesus under my breath. The idea of living with a bullet inside me was strange, but at least I was alive.

The doctor's calm tone gave me a sense of trust I hadn't felt since the accident. He asked me to roll onto my stomach so he could check another fragment lodged near my rib. Every movement sent ripples of pain through my back, but I complied, trusting that this was part of the path forward. The anesthesiologist arrived. He moved with quiet confidence, introducing himself with a firm but kind voice. He explained he would numb the area so the doctor could remove the smaller fragment.

His steady tone reminded me of how fragile everything still was, yet his composure brought me comfort. As the anesthesia spread through my back, the burning pain melted into a strange, tingling warmth. My body felt heavy but still free of the stabbing ache that had consumed me for hours. I exhaled, feeling my nerves loosen for the first time. Because my injury involved a firearm, the doctor explained that law enforcement had to be notified.

Before I could even process that, a police officer entered. The air within tightens. His black uniform was crisp, his expression was unreadable. He carried a notepad in one hand, a pen in the other, his presence all business. "Steven, is that your name?" he asked. "I go by Steve," I replied, "but my official name is Steven." "Is that with a V or a PH?" "With a V," I said, my voice steady even though my heart was still pounding. He nodded, jotting it down. "And your last name?" "Hauer, H-A-U-E-R." The officer looked up from his pad, his eyes softening. "Date of birth?" "May 9, 1969," I said. He raised an eyebrow. "Sixteen?" I nodded.

"All right, Steve," he replied. "What transpired?" "My best friend Kurt Simon is fifteen, and my nephew Chris Hauer is thirteen. We were scouting for squirrels in the woods. Not hunting, just looking for signs before the season opened next weekend." The words came out, each one heavy. I desired him to know the truth, rather than just headlines. "So you were just scouting," he repeated, confirming. "Yes. We weren't shooting anything. Just looking," I said. "We were checking where they nest. I guess we didn't think about how close we were standing or what could happen." He wrote a few notes, then looked back up. His tone softened. "Thank you for being honest, Steve. Just be more careful next time."

When he left, I felt a wave of exhaustion hit me. The room grew quiet again except for the faint buzz of medical equipment. I thought about what he'd said. Take care. The doctor returned, his gloved hands ready. "The numbing medicine has taken hold," he said. "Lets remove that piece." A few moments later, I heard the metallic clink of the bullet fragment landing in a tray. "Steve," he uttered with amusement, "you wish to keep it?" I managed a weak laugh. "No, thank you. I've had enough reminders." Still, as he threw it away, I felt a brief flicker of regret. Maybe keeping it would've made what happened feel more real, something I could hold in my hand. Instead, I just carried it in memory.

The doctor closed the wound with ten careful stitches, covering it with a fresh bandage. Every movement tugged, but I stayed still. When he finished, he gave a small nod of approval. "That's it. You did good." I asked, "How long will I have to stay?" He glanced at the chart. "We'll move you to intensive care tonight, just to monitor you. If everything looks good, you'll go to a regular room tomorrow." Relief and fatigue mingled inside me. I closed my eyes and let out a shaky breath. For the first time since the accident, I felt safe. The worst situation had passed, for now. As the lights dimmed and the hospital quieted, I whispered another prayer. "Thank you, Lord," I mumbled. "One inch. One chance. I won't waste it."

A Night in Intensive Care

The nurse guided me out of the hospital room and onto the gurney. The cool metal beneath me sent a shiver through my body, a cold contrast to the heat of pain radiating from my back. The ceiling lights above flashed as we moved, their glow reflecting off the polished tiles like passing stars. Each bend in the corridor felt like a struggle. The gurney rattled over uneven seams in the floor, and every bump jolted through me like a reminder of how fragile I'd become. I gripped the edge of the blanket, trying to steady myself, my breath coming in shallow bursts.

The antiseptic smell of the corridor filled the air, sharp and clean, almost too clean. It mixed with the faint scent of latex gloves and alcohol wipes, the unmistakable smell of a hospital at night. When we reached the elevator, the nurse pressed the button with calm precision. I watched her movements, so methodical, so gentle, yet I could sense the urgency behind her quiet focus. The elevator doors opened with a soft chime, and as we rolled inside, the hum of the machinery surrounding me. The gentle upward pull made my stomach twist. My body ached from the motion, but the nurse stayed beside me, one hand resting on my shoulder, a slight gesture that offered a surprising amount of comfort. With the opening, a fresh domain presented itself. The lights were dimmer here, the air cooler.

The intensive care unit carried a quiet intensity, a stillness that seemed to hum with hidden life. Nurses moved but, their shoes whispering across the floor. Machines beeped, a rhythm that filled the silence like a strange heartbeat. I was rolled into a small room filled with glowing screens and tubes. The nurses sprang into action, their teamwork effortless, almost rehearsed. One adjusted the IV lines while another checked the monitors. The icy touch of an alcohol swab brushed against my skin, followed by the sharp sting of a needle. I winced but said nothing. I was too tired, too aware that these strangers were now the ones keeping me alive.

As the monitors beeped in steady patterns, I stared at the numbers, heart rate, oxygen, blood pressure, each one a code for how close I was to the edge. It was both comforting and terrifying. Hours passed in fragments. I drifted between awareness and exhaustion, the beeping of machines mixing with distant murmurs in the hallway.

A soft tone then cut through the fog. "Your parents are here," the nurse said. Those words pulled me back. I tried to straighten up, ignoring the sharp pain that cut through my back. When they entered, I could see the worry written all over their faces. My mother's eyes glistened as she tried to smile, and my father stood close behind her, his jaw tight, his hands shoved deep in his pockets like he was holding himself together by sheer will. "I'm okay," I whispered, forcing a small grin. "It hurts, but I'm okay." My mom reached for my hand. Her skin felt warm, and her thumb brushed the top of mine in gentle circles. "The doctor said you need to rest," she whispered. "No more trying to do too much. Just rest and heal." I nodded, her words echoing the doctor's advice earlier that day.

The event settled upon my chest, this happening for the initial instance since the mishap. I wasn't invincible. I wasn't even close. With the departure of my parents, pledging to return when morning arrived, quietude once again settled. The hallway sounds faded, replaced by the hum of machines and the faint hiss of oxygen. Gazing at the ceiling, I traced minor paint cracks, offering thanks to God, not for freedom from suffering, but for his presence. For having another chance. During the night, I must have drifted.

When I opened my eyes, daylight filtered through the blinds in pale strips. The nurse entered with a kind smile. "Good morning," she said. "A priest is here today, offering prayers for patients. Would you like him to stop by?" "Yes," I said. "Please." There was no hesitation in my voice. I wanted those prayers. I needed them. She adjusted my blankets as I waited, her touch careful, almost reverent. A few minutes later, the priest stepped into the room, wearing a simple stole and holding a small prayer book. His presence brought a calm that words can't quite explain. He prayed over me, his voice low and steady, asking for healing and peace. As he spoke, I closed my eyes. The discomfort remained, yet it became

45

unimportant then. I felt surrounded, not through machines nor dread, however via faith, through affection, through something bigger than the hospital confines nearby.

Later that morning, the nurse returned. "You're doing great," she said. "We'll be moving you to a regular room soon." She began removing the IV lines, one by one. Each release felt like shedding a layer of confinement. The constant beeping stopped, replaced by silence, real silence. For the first time since arriving, I could breathe. The sense of freedom was overwhelming, almost sacred. I whispered another quiet thank-you, this time to God, for getting me this far. This journey continued, yet forward motion occurred, one minor achievement each instance.

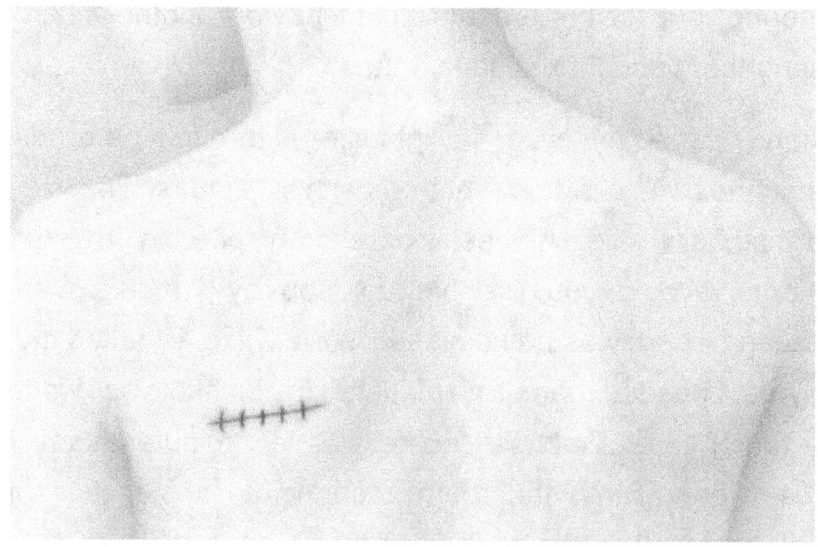

First Entry point of the bullet and the stitches used to close the wound.

Transferring to A Regular Hospital Bed

After a brief wait, the nurse appeared beside my bed with a calm smile. "Ready to move to your new room?" she asked. I nodded, grateful to be leaving the constant noise of the intensive-care unit. As she pushed the gurney through the corridor, the beeping monitors and hurried footsteps faded behind us. The air grew quieter, softer. Halting at my new dwelling's entrance, I experienced a surge of relief. A basic room contained only one window and a delicate scent of cleaning liquid. The absence of humming machines felt almost unreal. For the first time in days, I could hear my breathing.

I pondered how far I had traveled, how near I had come to being absent, as I settled into my bed. Hope, fragile but alive, hope rose inside me. While I was settling in, my parish priest, Father Elgar, was scouring the hospital trying to find me. Later I learned he had checked every floor and every nurse's station before finally spotting my name outside the new room. When he walked in, his face lit up. "Steve, I've been looking for you everywhere!" he said with a relieved laugh. "They wasted no time in moving you from intensive care." I smiled, feeling the warmth of familiarity. "They sure didn't," I said. He set his Bible on the table and pulled a chair close to the bed. "Let's pray," he whispered. Together we made the sign of the cross, his voice gentle but full of conviction. The words of his prayer filled the quiet room, washing over me like sunlight breaking through clouds. When he finished, he squeezed my hand and looked at his watch. "I wish I could stay longer," he said with regret. "But I have to get to Mala Strana nursing home for Mass." "Thank you, Father," I said. "You found me just when I needed that." He smiled, gave me a final blessing, and slipped out.

The room felt lighter after he left, a calm, holy stillness lingering in the air. After a while, I grew aware of the ticking clock beside my bed. It had been nearly half an hour since the last nurse had come in. Just as I wondered if they had forgotten about me, the door opened. A cheerful nurse stepped in, carrying a clipboard. "Hungry for lunch?" she asked. I laughed. "You have no idea." She grinned. "Good. I'll bring it right up." An hour later she returned with a tray, setting it on the table. The smell alone was enough to lift my spirits. I ate every bite, not because it was gourmet food, but because it meant I was healing.

Midway through lunch, the door opened again. My mom and dad entered, smiling wide. Their faces carried the exhaustion of sleepless nights but also a new brightness, relief. My mom told me the nurses had arranged everything for a smooth discharge the following afternoon. I was thankful for their care, though part of me ached to go home that very moment. When they left, the silence settled in again. Boredom crept over me, heavier than before. I stared at the ceiling, counting the dots on the tiles.

Then I spotted the small television mounted in the corner. After a few minutes of fumbling with the buttons, I found the remote and turned it on. The screen flickered to life, filling the room with color and sound. I scrolled through channels, amazed by the variety. Back home, our old set had no remote and only a handful of channels. Here, there were dozens. It felt like luxury. I leaned back, losing myself in the simple joy of it, grateful for a distraction that didn't involve needles or monitors.

After a couple of hours, a knock at the door. "Come in!" I called. The door swung open, and there stood Joe, my brother-in-law, with Chris and Kurt right behind him. "Hello there, Buckshot! Lead Foot! How are you doing?" Joe's booming voice filled the room. I laughed in disbelief. "What are you guys doing here?" Joe explained that the boys hadn't slept at all the night before. "Kurt called me around 1a.m.," he said. "He was worried sick. So after school I told them I'd bring them to see you."

I looked over at Kurt. His eyes were tired, his shoulders tense. "I just couldn't stop thinking about it," he whispered. "I kept seeing it happen. I threw up a few times. I barely slept for two hours." Hearing that broke something open inside me. I hadn't realized how much the accident had shaken him too. "Hey," I said softly, "I'm okay. Really. You don't have to carry that." He nodded, still fighting the weight of guilt. Gratitude welled up inside me. Despite everything, he was here, loyal, caring, still my friend. We talked for a long while, replaying the day, trying to make sense of it together. Each word seemed to heal a little more of what fear had broken.

Just as they were about to leave, the door burst open again. My brothers, John and Tony, stepped in, their energy filling the room instantly. Laughter erupted as they teased me about the hospital gown and the television remote I was gripping like treasure. The tension of the past days melted away in that moment. I could see the relief on their faces as we talked. I was alive, breathing, joking. I walked them through what had happened, every detail, and we all knew how differently it could have ended. Tony leaned forward and said quietly, "We definitely had a guardian angel watching over us." He was right. Surrounded by my family and friends, I felt it too. God had been there through every second, through fear, through pain, through the impossible miracle of survival. That night, as the lights dimmed, and the hospital grew still, I whispered one more prayer of thanks. Tomorrow I would leave this place behind, but the lessons it gave me would stay forever.

Released from the Hospital

I woke to the soft rustle of footsteps and the faint clatter of a breakfast tray. The nurse stood by my bed, smiling. "Good morning, Steve. How are we feeling today?" Still half asleep, I blinked against the morning light and mumbled something close to "tired but okay." She chuckled and handed me the breakfast menu. My mind was groggy, my body heavy, but the realization that it was my last morning here stirred something hopeful inside me. After placing my order, I sank back into the pillow, drifting in and out of light sleep until the smell of food brought me awake. The eggs and toast weren't anything special, but to me, it felt like freedom on a plate. Every bite was one step closer to going home.

Once I finished eating, I reached for the remote and turned on the television. The bright flicker of the screen filled the quiet room, with the familiar sounds of a theme song echoing through the air. For a moment, I forgot about hospitals and IVs and the sterile smell of disinfectant. I just watched, letting my mind rest on something simple and normal.

Not long after, the door opened again, and the nurse returned with the lunch menu. "You're making the most of your last day, huh?" she said. Before I could answer, the door opened once more, and there she was. My mom. She stepped in with a familiar mix of love and determination in her eyes. The harsh fluorescent light softened in her presence. "Good morning, honey," she said, her voice gentle but steady. Just hearing her voice made my chest loosen. "Hey, Mom," I said, smiling. "Are you ready to break me out of here?" She laughed, shaking her head. "You have no idea." Her timing couldn't have been better.

The nurse came back moments later with the discharge papers in hand. "Looks like we're all set," she said. "As soon as you finish eating, we'll get you on your way." "Great!" I said. My mom chuckled but kept glancing at the clock. "Hurry and finish up, Steve," she urged, half teasing, half impatient. I could see the relief on her face, she wanted this chapter closed as much as I did.

When I was done, I swung my legs over the edge of the bed and began changing into my clothes. The feeling of wearing something that wasn't a hospital gown was incredible. Every movement reminded me I was leaving behind the tubes, the monitors, and the endless hum of machines. "I can walk," I said as the nurse rolled in a wheelchair. She smiled. "I believe you, but it's hospital policy. We wheel everyone out." I sighed but didn't argue. Sitting down,

I realized how symbolic this moment was, not weakness, but transition. As she pushed me down the hall, I took one last look around. The sterile white walls that had surrounded me for days now seemed softer, almost friendly. They had seen me at my weakest and carried me to safety. The wheels squeaked as we turned the corner toward the exit. The smell of fresh air grew stronger, and sunlight spilled through the glass doors ahead. My heart started racing.

When we reached the entrance, my mom's car pulled up to the curb. She was smiling from ear to ear, her eyes bright with gratitude and relief. The nurse locked the brakes, handed her a form, and wished me well. "Take care of yourself, Steve," she said. "I will," I replied, meaning every word. My mom stepped out and opened the passenger door. "Come on," she whispered. "Let's go home." As I stood and slid into the seat, the hospital faded behind me. The doors closed, and with them, a long and painful chapter. The hum of the car engine sounded like freedom. As we pulled away, I looked out the window. The world outside was more vivid than I remembered, the sky bluer, the trees brighter, life itself somehow louder. For the first time since the accident, I wasn't thinking about what I'd lost. I was thinking about what I still had: life, faith, family, and a second chance.

Recovery at Home Day One

Recovery at home was peaceful but boring. I tried to follow the doctor's orders as best I could, spending most of my time stretched out on the couch with my back supported by a stack of pillows. The stillness of the house was almost eerie after the constant hum and activity of the hospital. There was not much to do. Back then, we did not have cable or satellite television. Our family relied on the old rooftop antenna, the kind that turned with a loud metallic click when you tried to tune it. On a good day, we might pick up five of the seven available channels, though the picture often danced with static. When it rained, the screen turned to snow. There were no cell phones, no internet, and no easy way to pass the time. If I wanted to talk to my friends, it meant making a long distance call, and those were expensive. We lived out in the countryside near New Prague, but most of my friends were in Montgomery, about seven miles away. Every phone call across that invisible town line added up, and every visit meant biking miles down gravel roads, something the doctor had forbidden. So I stayed home, stuck between boredom and restlessness.

I did not even have a video game console to keep me busy. The house was quiet except for the ticking of the wall clock and the low hum of the refrigerator. I tried to read, though I could never focus for long. The television offered little relief. Daytime shows were filled with soap opera drama that did not interest me. Each day dragged on, slow and predictable.

By Tuesday afternoon I felt like I was going stir crazy. I lay there on the couch staring at the ceiling, imagining the freedom of being back at school, surrounded by friends and noise. I broke down and begged my parents. "Please," I said. "Can I go back to school tomorrow, just for a little while?" They exchanged a look, that quiet parental conversation that does not need words. My dad shook his head. "Not yet, Steve. You need a few more days to rest." Disappointment sank in like a stone. I wanted to argue, but I knew they were right.

My body still ached, and every time I shifted I was reminded of how fragile I still was. Sometime later, while I lay on the couch flipping between the few clear channels, I heard a deep rumble outside. It started faint, like distant thunder, then grew louder until the dishes in the cupboard rattled. I sat up and looked out the window. Five massive semis were pulling into our yard, each hauling a load of building materials. My pulse quickened, the first genuine excitement I had felt in days.

They were here to begin construction of our new home. I pressed my face against the glass as the trucks parked in a long row across the gravel driveway. The morning sun glinted off the metal frames as the drivers climbed down from their cabs. Within minutes, the quiet of the countryside gave way to clanging chains, the whir of engines, and the shouts of the crew as they unloaded. The sight was mesmerizing. Our family had decided to build a new house next to the one we were living in. My sister Jane and her husband Joe were buying the old farmhouse and would keep the land as part of the family farm. That place held deep roots, generations of sweat, faith, and pride. My great great grandfather had purchased the land from the United States government for just one dollar an acre. My dad always said it was not about money, it was about keeping the family name tied to the soil that had provided for us for so long.

Now, watching the heavy equipment move across the field, I could see that determination alive in him. The hydraulic arms lifted massive beams, lowering them into place. The ground shook beneath the weight of the excavator as it roared to life, its metal teeth biting into the earth. Clouds of dust billowed up, catching the sunlight in golden streaks. I stood by the kitchen window, transfixed. The smell of turned soil mixed with the smell of diesel from the trucks. For the first time since the accident, I felt a spark of excitement instead of fear. This was something new, something hopeful. Each scoop of dirt carved out established not just a house but a new beginning. I could almost see it, the walls rising, the roof forming, laughter echoing through painted rooms. Our old house had held memories of the past, but this one would hold the promise of everything still to come. As I watched the crew work with steady rhythm and purpose, I felt gratitude building inside me. Life was still fragile, still uncertain, but it was moving forward, and so were we.

Recovery at Home Day Two

With a delicious breakfast completed, I put on my jacket and went outside to witness the impressive sight of the building crew constructing our new home. I couldn't believe that only a few months earlier my parents had completed all the details, including the ambitious promise that the house would be completed in five to seven days. The idea seemed almost impossible to me. I had seen other homes take months to finish, yet here it was, coming together before my eyes with astonishing speed. Anticipation bubbled inside me as I watched the workers maneuver materials into place. Every movement was precise and purposeful. The cranes lifted large sections of the house from the semis, and the workers guided them, securing each piece with practiced ease. The entire scene filled me with awe.

Exciting witnessing this transformation was unlike anything I had ever experienced. By midday, the building crew had made incredible progress. The walls were up, and the house was taking shape. I spoke with one of the crew members, unable to hide my enthusiasm. He smiled and told me that the next day would be even more exciting. They planned to install the finished bathroom and complete the rest of the structure, including the roof. The thought of seeing the skeleton of the house turn into a complete home filled me with energy and hope.

That evening, the warm glow of the kitchen lights wrapped around us as my parents, my brother in law Joe, and my sister Jane gathered around the old wooden table. The aroma of a home cooked meal filled the room, creating a feeling of comfort and belonging. I could hardly contain myself as I began telling them everything that had happened. With wide eyes and animated hands, I described how the crew had used a massive crane to lift entire sections of the house from the semis and set them perfectly into place. I told them I had spent hours standing nearby, asking endless questions and watching each movement. My family laughed as I spoke, their amusement at my curiosity blending with the soft clinking of silverware. In that cozy kitchen, surrounded by love and laughter, I felt gratitude swell inside me. The old house had seen its share of long days and hard work, but now, we were building something new. It felt symbolic, a reflection of the healing taking place both inside me and within our family.

Later that evening, as the sun dipped below the horizon and painted the kitchen in shades of orange and gold, my parents turned their attention to me. Concern showed on their faces. My mom's gentle eyes studied me carefully as she asked about my recovery.

"How's your back today? Any pain or headaches?" she asked softly. I assured her I was feeling better, stronger than the day before. The pain had faded to a dull ache, and I was eager to get back to normal life. But her worry didn't fade. She pressed a little further, asking about my plans for the next day.

I told her I wanted to watch the construction again and maybe help our neighbors, Roman and Hilmar, with chores on their second farm. My mom smiled but shook her head. "Not yet, Steve. You're still healing. No lifting over twenty pounds," she said firmly. I tried to laugh it off, but deep down, I knew she was right. Her love was fierce, protective, and grounded in wisdom. I promised her I would be careful and let Roman and Hilmar know about the restrictions.

The rest of the evening unfolded peacefully. Laughter returned to the table, soft conversation mingling with the fading light. I realized how blessed I was to have such firm support surrounding me. My parents' guidance, my siblings' encouragement, and the quiet love that filled our home reminded me that healing was more than physical. It was emotional, too. When my parents told me I could stay home one more day before returning to school on Friday, I felt a surge of happiness. I will watch the progress again tomorrow.

The thought of seeing the roof take shape and the walls close in around the structure filled me with excitement. That night, as I lay in bed, my mind replayed the day's images. I pictured the walls rising higher, the roof beams falling into place, and sunlight shining through the open frames. I imagined walking through our new home when it was finished, feeling the smooth wooden floors under my feet, hearing laughter echo through the halls. Gratitude filled me as I closed my eyes.

The next morning, I woke early, eager for the sound of trucks arriving. Sitting at the kitchen table, I poured myself a bowl of cereal and looked out the window toward the west, where our dream home stood against the morning sky. The sun's first light stretched across the field, casting a golden glow on the half built walls.

I could already hear a faint rumble of engines in the distance. Moments later, the construction crew pulled up, ready for another long day. Their voices carried through the air as they unloaded tools and equipment. The smell of sawdust and diesel mixed with the cool morning breeze. I quickly slipped on my jacket and ran outside to watch.

The same crewman I had spoken with before greeted me with a grin. "You made it back," he said. "Today's the big day. The bathroom unit goes in first, then the roof." I could hardly contain my excitement. He explained how the bathroom had been prefabricated at the factory and would be lifted into place by the crane in one piece, forming the heart of the house. I stood there, completely fascinated as the crane roared to life, its cable tightening as it lifted the massive section through the air. Piece by piece, the rest of the house came together around it. Walls, beams, and the panels all slid into place as if they had been waiting for this exact moment.

I could feel the energy of creation in the air, the hum of teamwork and purpose. As evening arrived, the sun sank low once again, coating the house in shades of amber. My parents arrived with Jane and Joe, and the look on their faces said everything. Pride, relief, and gratitude all at once.

We gathered inside what would soon be our kitchen, standing on the bare plywood floor as if it were already home. Later that night, back at the dinner table, I told them every detail. I described how the crew had pieced together the house like a puzzle, how each movement had fit perfectly. My family listened intently, their laughter and excitement matching my own. In that warm kitchen, surrounded by the people I loved most, I felt something greater than excitement. I felt grace. The simple joy of being alive, of being together, of watching something grow from the ground up, both a home and a second chance.

Recovery at Home Day Three

Thursday morning arrived with a quiet sense of excitement. It would be my last day at home before returning to school, and I could feel the anticipation buzzing through me from the moment I opened my eyes. The house was still and peaceful, with the faint light of dawn slipping through the curtains. I sat at the kitchen table and poured myself a bowl of cereal.

For a moment I just sat there, spoon in hand, watching the steam rise from the coffeepot and listening to the familiar sounds of the house waking up. I looked out the window to the west, where the skeleton of our new home stood against the pale sky. With each passing day, it looked more like a house and less like a construction site. As I ate, I thought about everything that had happened over the past week. The fear, the pain, the prayers, and the slow climb back toward health. Now, sitting there in the morning quiet, it felt almost like a dream. The accident, the hospital, the surgery that never happened, the long nights in bed, all of it seemed distant.

What was real now was this, the sound of hammers, the smell of sawdust, and exciting new beginnings. Then I saw them. The construction crew's trucks appeared one by one, their headlights cutting through the morning mist. My heart skipped a beat. I set down my spoon, grabbed my jacket, and ran out the door. The cold air held the aroma of dirt and wood. The workers were already unloading their equipment, their laughter echoing across the yard. The rhythmic clatter of hammers began, followed by the low hum of the generator. The smell of sawdust mixed with the crisp morning air. It was a symphony of creation. I stood there, watching in awe as the structure continued to rise. Each beam lifted into place was a minor miracle. Every nail driven in felt like progress, not just for the house but for all of us. The day moved quickly.

By afternoon, the frame of the house looked nearly complete. The sun hung high, bathing the site in golden light. I could see the vision of our future home taking shape, room by room. My chest swelled with pride knowing that this place, built with such care and precision, would soon hold the laughter, warmth, and memories of our family. As the sun sank toward the horizon, a soft orange glow fell across the site. I could not stop smiling. Soon, my parents' car came up the driveway, with Jane and Joe following close behind. The weariness on their faces faded as they stepped out and looked at the progress. Their smiles mirrored mine. We stood together, taking in the sight of our dream home rising from the ground. My mom's eyes glistened as she whispered, "It's really happening." That evening, we gathered in the kitchen of our old house, the heart of so many memories. The aroma of stew filled the air as we sat around the worn wooden table that had seen decades of family meals. The laughter and chatter that filled the room carried a feeling of gratitude and hope.

I told them about everything that had happened that day, the steady pace of the crew, the teamwork, the way the walls had gone up like pieces of a puzzle. My excitement spilled out in every word, and my family smiled at my enthusiasm. At that moment, I realized that home was not just a place being built outside. It was right there around that table. After dinner, my mom contemplated me. "How's your back?" she asked. "Any pain or headaches?" I smiled. "Better than ever," I said honestly. The stiffness had eased, and the pain that once kept me awake at night was now little more than a dull reminder. Still, she kept her eyes on me, studying me carefully as only a mother can. "You seem stronger," she said, then added softly, "I think it's time." "Time for what?" I asked, though I already knew. Her smile widened. "Time to go back to school. You don't want to fall behind on your work." For a moment I just sat there, letting her words sink in. Returning to school. It felt strange after everything that had happened, yet it also felt right. I was ready. A wave of mixed feelings washed over me, nervousness, excitement, curiosity. I thought of my friends, my teachers, and the familiar rhythm of school life. I could almost hear the hallway chatter, the echo of lockers closing, the normalcy I had longed for.

That night, I packed my backpack with care, placing my books and folders neatly inside. I laid out my clothes for the next morning, my heart light with anticipation. When I turned off the light and crawled into bed, I stared at the ceiling for a while, my mind racing with thoughts of the days ahead. Tomorrow I will return to school. Tomorrow I will walk back into my life. The house outside was still unfinished, but like me, it was coming together one day at a time. As sleep overtook me, I whispered a silent prayer of gratitude. I thanked God for my healing, for my family, and for the simple gift of tomorrow.

Back to School and Reality

Friday morning arrived with a rush of mixed emotions. Excitement, nervousness, and curiosity all stirred inside me as I woke to the soft glow of morning light filtering through the window. I was going back to school. After days of recovery at home, I was ready to rejoin my friends and step back into normal life, though part of me wondered how different it might feel after everything that had happened. I made my way to the kitchen, the smell of toast and coffee already filling the air. As I poured myself a bowl of cereal, I found my eyes drifting to the clock on the wall. The steady tick of its second hand echoed through the quiet kitchen. Each sound seemed to build my anticipation a little more.

After breakfast, I grabbed my backpack and jacket, double-checking that I had everything I needed. When I stepped outside, a cool gust of autumn air brushed against my face, waking me up. I breathed, savoring the freshness. The sky was streaked with pale orange as the sun rose, and for the first time in a long while, I felt a sense of excitement about the unknown. As I waiting for the bus, I could hear the faint hum of traffic in the distance. The air was crisp, carrying the faint scent of damp leaves and earth. Then, right on schedule, the bright yellow bus appeared at the end of the road. Its engine rumbled as it pulled up, and the doors creaked open with a familiar hiss.

Climbing aboard, I found my usual seat and sank into it with a mix of comfort and anticipation. As the bus rolled through the countryside, the landscape outside was painted in shades of green and gold. The rhythmic motion of the ride, the chatter of students, and the faint smell of diesel all felt comforting. Despite my nerves, I could not help but smile. I was on my way back to the life I had missed. When the bus stopped in front of the school, I stepped out and inhaled deeply the scent of fresh air and the earthy aroma of Green Giant silage drifting from a nearby silage mound. It reminds me back to my childhood, reminding me of walking those same fields near home. The walk to the entrance felt surreal. I had imagined this moment for days, but now that it was here, I realized I did not have a class schedule. The thought made me chuckle to myself.

I pushed open the front door and headed straight to the main office. The school secretary looked up from her desk with a kind smile. "Steve," she said, "I am so glad to see you." Her voice carried a mix of surprise and relief. Before I could even ask about my schedule, she leaned forward and whispered, "I heard you got shot in the back. What happened?" The question caught me off guard. For a moment, I just stared at her, then laughed. "It was a big misunderstanding," I blurted. "I'm okay now." Her expression softened as she let out a sigh of relief. "Well, thank God for that," she said. We both laughed, and I received my schedule before heading down the hallway toward my first class.

The bell rang just as I stepped into the room. The familiar sound filled me with both nostalgia and adrenaline. Students were shuffling into their seats, talking over one another, until the teacher's voice boomed over the noise. He began calling roll, his deep voice echoing off the classroom walls. When he reached my name, the room fell silent. Every head turned toward me. "Steve Hauer," he said slowly, his expression changing from focus to shock. "Where have you been? I heard you were shot." I froze, unsure how to respond. My classmates stared, eyes wide, waiting for me to confirm the rumor. I managed a small, uneasy smile. "I'm fine," I said simply. "Just happy to be back." The tension broke instantly. A few kids laughed awkwardly. Others leaned over their desks, whispering to each other.

The teacher nodded, visibly relieved. "Well," he said with a grin, "we're just glad you're here." That same scene repeated throughout the day. Every classroom brought new questions, new reactions, and more laughter. By lunchtime, the story had already made its way around the school. Everywhere I went, people were whispering, trying to piece together what had actually happened. I could feel curiosity in every hallway I passed.

By mid afternoon, I felt the strain of the long day. My back ached slightly, though I tried not to show it. As the last class ended, I hurried down the hall toward the restroom. Just as I reached for the door, I heard someone call out. "Steve! Wait up!" It was my friend George, one of the guys I used to hang out with during lunch. He jogged up beside me, grinning. "Man, it's good to see you. I heard all kinds of wild stories about you." Before I could respond, his eyes narrowed at something on my back. "Hey, what's that?" he asked. Before I could stop him, he reached out and touched the spot beneath my shirt where the wound had been stitched. Pain shot through me, and I let out a sharp scream. George jumped back in shock. "What in the world, man?" he said, his eyes wide. I took a breath, trying to calm down. "George, don't do that again," I said firmly. "That's where I got shot last week." His face went pale. "You're serious?" I nodded. "Yeah. A point twenty two rifle. It was an accident, but it's still there." He blinked, his shock giving way to disbelief. "I thought that was just some crazy rumor." "Not anymore," I said with a faint smile. The bell rang, cutting our conversation short. We both laughed awkwardly, promising to talk more later.

As I walked back to class, the tension eased, replaced by a strange sense of relief. That day had been filled with more surprises than I expected. There was laughter, disbelief, and even a little pain, but there was also something else, normalcy. I was back where I belonged, surrounded by familiar faces and everyday chaos. When I finally got home that afternoon, I dropped my backpack on the floor and collapsed onto the couch. My mom looked over from the kitchen and smiled. "So," she said, "how was your first day back?" I thought for a moment, then smiled back. "Different," I said, "but good." As I leaned back and closed my eyes, I realized how true that was. Life would never be quite the same again, but maybe that was okay. I had survived the unthinkable. I was healing, learning, and moving forward. Tomorrow would be another day, another step back into the world I was lucky enough to still be part of.

Final Thoughts

The last bell rang, echoing through the halls and marking the end of another school week. As the sound faded, a wave of relief washed over me. It was Friday, and for the first time in a long while, I could relax. I strolled down the corridor, my backpack slung over one shoulder, my steps light with exhaustion and gratitude. The chatter of students filled the air, laughter spilling from every direction, but my thoughts were elsewhere. I kept thinking about everything that had happened since my return, the whispers, the curious stares, the unexpected concern in people's voices. Throughout the day, classmates and teachers alike had approached me, each one asking how I was doing. Their words were filled with genuine care, and it surprised me how deeply their kindness touched me. I had never thought of myself as someone people paid much attention to. I kept to myself, quiet and focused.

Yet now, as one person after another stopped to talk, to ask, or even just to smile, I realized something important. People cared. That simple truth hit me harder than I expected. Beneath all the noise and confusion of school life, there were hearts that noticed, friends that cared, and teachers who remembered. For the first time, I saw that my life was connected to others in ways I had never understood before.

As I stepped outside, the crisp air of late afternoon greeted me. The sky stretched wide above, streaked with orange and gold as the sun began its descent. I breathed, feeling peace settle over me. Walking toward the bus, I glanced back at the school building. Its windows glowed in the fading light, and I felt a quiet sense of closure. This place, these halls, these people, had become part of my journey. I climbed the bus steps and took my seat by the window. As the engine started and the bus rumbled forward, my thoughts turned inward. The rhythm of the tires against the road became a soft background to the memories that played in my mind. The sound of that gunshot. The flash of pain. The fear that followed.

Even now, it did not seem real. The bullet had missed my heart by an inch. An inch that separated life from death. That thought never left me. Each time I remembered it, a chill ran through me, followed by a flood of gratitude so strong it almost brought me to tears. I had survived something that should have ended my life. There was no other way to explain it except through faith. God had spared me. I did not understand why. Maybe I never would. But deep down, I knew it was not a chance. It had a purpose. As the bus carried me down the familiar country roads toward home, I gazed out the window at the fields stretching into the distance.

The evening light shimmered over them, and the quiet hum of the engine seemed to blend with my thoughts. Was there a reason I was still here? Was there something I did? The questions circled in my mind, but instead of fear, I felt peace.

I believed with all my heart that God had guided me through that day for a reason. Maybe that reason was as simple as telling my story. Maybe it was to remind others of how precious life is, or how faith can carry us through the darkest moments. Whatever the reason, I knew one thing for certain, my life had changed forever. That near tragedy had opened my eyes to things I had taken for granted. The beauty of an ordinary sunrise. The warmth of a family dinner. The laughter of friends. The simple gift of breath in my lungs and a heartbeat in my chest. As the bus turned down the last stretch of road toward home, I leaned my head against the window and closed my eyes. The hum of the engine and the steady rhythm of the ride lulled me into calm reflection. I whispered a quiet prayer of thanks, my words soft but sincere. I thanked God for my second chance, for my family, for every small grace I had once overlooked. I knew the road ahead would not always be easy, but I was ready for it. I had been given life again, and I intended to live it with purpose, with gratitude, and with faith. Because sometimes, it only takes one inch between life and death to change everything.

Verses That Helped Me Through My Journey

Here are powerful verses from the TEV wording (Today's English Version / Good News Bible) These verses spoke to me because they remind me that no matter how difficult life gets, God is close, God strengthens us, and God never abandons us. When I needed direction, these verses gave me clarity. When I needed peace, they calmed my mind. When I felt weak, they reminded me that Christ gives me strength. My hope is that these verses speak to you the same way they spoke to me.

I have the strength to face all conditions by the power that Christ gives me.

Psalm 46:1

God is our shelter and strength, always ready to help in times of trouble.

Isaiah 41:10

Do not be afraid, I am with you. I am your God, let nothing terrify you. I will make you strong and help you.

Matthew 11:28

Come to me, all of you who are tired from carrying heavy loads, and I will give you rest.

John 14:27

Peace is what I leave with you. It is my own peace that I give you.

1 Peter 5:7

Leave all your worries with him, because he cares for you.

Jeremiah 29:11

I alone know the plans I have for you, plans to bring you prosperity and not disaster, plans to bring about the future you hope for.

Psalm 37:5

Give yourself to the Lord, trust in him, and he will help you.

Hebrews 13:5, 6

I will never leave you, I will never abandon you. The Lord is my helper.

Romans 8:28

We know that in all things God works for good with those who love him.

Isaiah 40:31

But those who trust in the Lord for help will find their strength renewed. They will rise on wings like eagles, they will run and not get weary, they will walk and not grow weak.

James 1:12

Happy are those who remain faithful under trials, because when they succeed in passing such a test, they will receive as their reward the life which God has promised to those who love him.

Romans 5:3, 4

We also boast of our troubles, because we know that trouble produces endurance, endurance brings God's approval, and his approval creates hope.

2 Corinthians 12:9

M grace is all you need, for my power is strongest when you are weak.

Galatians 6:9

So let us not become tired of doing good, for if we do not give up, the time will come when we will reap the harvest.

Hebrews 12:1

Let us run with determination the race that lies before us.

Psalm 29:11

The Lord gives strength to his people, the Lord blesses his people with peace.

2 Thessalonians 3:13

Do not get tired of doing what is good.

Psalm 55:22

Leave your troubles with the Lord, and he will defend you.

Philippians 4:7

And God's peace, which is far beyond human understanding, will keep your hearts and minds safe in union with Christ Jesus.

Philippians 4:7

Tools in Prayers That Helped Me Along My Journey

If life feels heavy right now and you're going through something hard, I want to share something that helped me in my darkest moments. Start by giving everything to Jesus Christ. Whatever you're facing, speak this prayer out loud ten times:

"Jesus, I entrust in you, take care of everything."

Say it with meaning. Let it come from your heart. If the fear or pressure comes back, don't be discouraged. That's just the enemy trying to stir doubt. Say the prayer again. Keep giving it back to God every time it tries to return. Keep going until peace settles in.

Another thing that brought me peace was learning how to silence the lies in your head (negative thoughts). When you hear that voice telling you you're not enough, that you're worthless, or that you don't matter, recognize that it is not from God. That voice is lying to you. When that happens, say this:

"In the name of Jesus Christ, I renounce the lie that [insert the lie]."

For example: "I renounce the lie that I'm a failure."

Speak it clearly and firmly. Keep doing this whenever those thoughts show up. Over time, you will feel peace take the place of those lies. This isn't just positive thinking. It is the truth of Christ restoring your spirit.

My Nightly Prayer:

Dear God, Thank You for giving me another day. I know you are not done with me yet. Help me to not take this for granted. Let me see that my life has purpose. Remind me that I matter, that I am enough, and that I am strong in you. Thank you for everything you have done for me. Amen.

My Other Nightly Prayer:

Dear God, I come before you at this moment. Please Enlighten what is dark in me, Strengthen what is weak in me, Mend what is broken in me, Heal what is sick in me, And revive whatever peace and love that has died in me. This prayer is for me, my family, my friends, my enemies and even those who hate me. Amen.

I'm sharing this because I've lived through it, and I know how powerful it is. These words changed my life, and I believe they can help you too.

Acknowledgments

Writing this book has been one of the most challenging and rewarding experiences of my life. It has required me to reopen old wounds, revisit painful memories, and find the courage to share moments I once thought I would never speak of again. But through it all, I have been reminded of how blessed I am to be surrounded by people who never stopped believing in me and who made this story possible.

First and foremost, I want to thank God for giving me a second chance at life and the strength to turn tragedy into purpose. Without His grace, I would not be here today. Every word in these pages is a reflection of His mercy and power.

To my mom and dad. You have both passed since I wrote this book. I know you are looking down on me and I know you are proud of me. Thank you for your love, patience, and guidance. You were with me from the moment of the accident through every painful hour of recovery and every step that followed. You showed me what real faith and unconditional love look like. Mom, your prayers carried me through nights when hope felt distant. Dad, your quiet strength taught me how to keep fighting.

To my family-my brothers John and Tony, my sister Jane, and my brother-in-law Joe-thank you for standing beside me during the hardest time of my life. Your visits, your laughter, and your belief that I would pull through gave me the will to keep going. Jane, I will never forget how fast you reacted that day. Your calm and strength under pressure helped save my life.

To my friends Kurt and Chris, I know this story has never been easy for any of us. We went through something no teenagers should ever experience. Yet through all the pain and guilt, you both stayed my friends. You showed courage, honesty, and loyalty when it mattered most. That means more to me than words can express.

To my teachers, especially Mr. Jackson and Ms. Foote-thank you for believing in me long before I ever believed in myself. You encouraged me to write when I thought I had nothing worth saying. The short story I wrote in your class became the foundation for this book. Your kindness and encouragement helped me discover a passion that would later define my purpose.

To every nurse, doctor, and medical worker who cared for me at Queen of Peace Hospital and St. Francis Hospital, thank you. Your compassion, patience, and skill made the difference between fear and comfort. You reminded me that healing is not just physical-it's also emotional and spiritual.

To the friends and community members who offered prayers, sent cards, and checked in on my family-you became part of my healing too. Every word, every gesture, and every prayer mattered more than you know.

To the readers holding this book, thank you for choosing to take this journey with me. My hope is that somewhere within these pages, you find encouragement, faith, and the reminder that no experience is wasted if it helps someone else find strength. If my story touches even one life, then everything I went through was worth it.

And finally, to my children—Jacob, Claire, and Nicholaus. You are my heart, my reason, and my legacy. Everything I do, I do for you. I want you to know that no matter what happens in life, faith will always light your path. Never forget that you are capable of overcoming anything through God's grace.

Thank you all—for your love, your faith, and your part in this miracle of life and purpose.

Steven A. Hauer.

Contributors

Darcy Sjomeling

Mike Sjomeling

Scott Linde

Barbie Linde

Mike Stifter

Kevin Dietrich

Jerry Tufvander

Andrew Buller-Russ

Brandon Fraser

James Hauer

Umairpublisher

Victoria Godnyuk

In the News

In the News

The New Prague Times

The Accident and Its Aftermath

After the accident, The New Prague Times published an article describing the event that changed my life. The story focused on the quick response of those nearby, the medical care that followed, and the lessons of firearm safety learned from that day.

Out of respect for my family's privacy, the full article is not reproduced here, but it served as an early reminder that a single moment can alter the course of a life forever. The coverage emphasized both the seriousness of the incident and the gratitude that followed. It became a lesson for the community about faith, responsibility, and the fragile line between life and loss.

Though the names of my family members appeared in that original story, the message that endures is far greater than the event itself. It is a reminder that survival often carries a purpose, and that purpose can inspire others long after the news fades from print.

The Montgomery Messenger

Young Author Earns Statewide Recognition

In 1987, *The Montgomery Messenger* published an article sharing much happier news.

Local Student Wins Writing Award and Scholarship

A Montgomery High School student has been recognized in The High School Writer of Minnesota competition for his essay "One Inch Between Life and Death," based on his real-life recovery from a near-fatal hunting accident.

Steven Hauer, a junior at Montgomery High School, earned the top writing honor and a ten-thousand-dollar scholarship to Jamestown College in North Dakota. His English teacher, Mr. Jackson, encouraged him to submit the story after reading it for class and noting its honesty and emotion.

"This story came straight from his heart," Mr. Jackson said. "It shows what courage and faith can do when life changes in an instant."

Steven credits his special education teacher, Ms. Foote, for helping him prepare the final version. "She made sure every word was clear, and every line was right," he said with a grin. "I even missed one period and quotation mark, but it turned out okay."

95

Principal McDermott praised the young writer, saying, "This achievement is something our entire school can be proud of. It proves that determination and creativity can take you far.

I had no plans of becoming a writer, intending instead to pursue a trade career. Yet that recognition became the spark that would one day grow into a full-length book sharing the same story with the world.

To the readers who picked Up this book, Thank You.

Your support means everything. I remember that every experience can help someone find hope or faith again.

I believe I'm a walking miracle. God kept me here for a reason, and I've taken that as a mission: to share my story and remind others that Jesus loves us all. If this book speaks to you, I hope you'll share it with someone who might need to hear it too.

One Inch. One Life. One Mission.

Book Club Discussion Guide

Book Club Discussion Guide

Created by Steven A. Hauer Thank you for choosing to read *One Inch Between Life and Death*. This story was written to inspire reflection, conversation, and gratitude for life's second chances. Whether you are reading it on your own or as part of a group, these questions are here to help guide thoughtful discussion. 1. What moment in Steven's story affected you the most, and why?

2. How did Steven's faith shape his ability to recover and find purpose after the accident?

3. What does "*One Inch Between Life and Death*" mean to you?

4. Have you ever experienced a time when faith, prayer, or hope helped you through something difficult?

5. How did Steven's family and community play a role in his healing?

6. What lessons about gratitude, responsibility, or safety stand out to you?

7. If you could ask Steven one question about his journey, what would it be?

8. How does this story make you think differently about the power of small decisions?

9. What message or emotion stayed with you the longest after finishing the book?

10. How might you share your own "one-inch moment" with others? Talk, reflect, and share. Every reader brings a different perspective, and together those insights can reveal new ways to see faith, purpose, and the value of life. Thank you again for reading.

Steven A. Hauer

Author Page

Steven A. Hauer's debut memoir, *One Inch Between Life and Death Updated and Revised Second Edition*, is a true story of survival, resilience, and rediscovery. After surviving a near fatal hunting accident, Steven was forced to reflect on the moments that shaped his life and to explore the meaning behind his second chance. He considers himself a walking miracle.

Through years of challenge and personal growth, Steven came to believe he was spared for a reason, to share his story and inspire others. One Inch Between Life and Death marks his first published memoir.

Steven enjoys spending time with his kids and friends, fishing, being outdoors, playing card games, and listening to music. He is also active as a volunteer with several organizations, where he continues to give back and support local causes.

www.ingramcontent.com/pod-product-compliance
Lightning Source LLC
Chambersburg PA
CBHW070638130626
46555CB00006B/2592